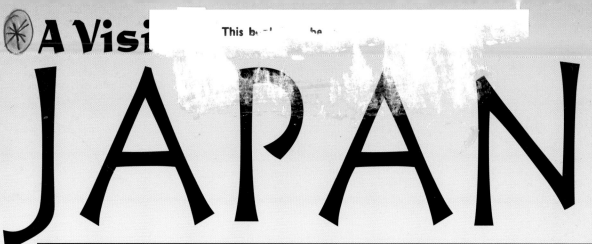

A Visi

JAPAN

This b

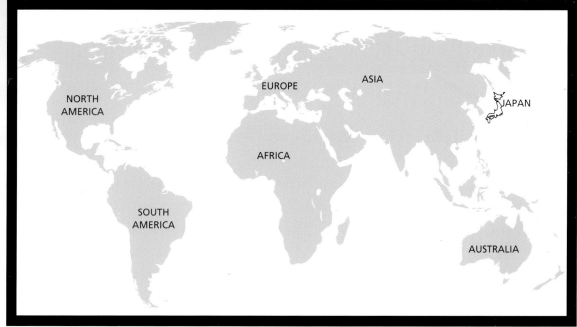

NORTH
AMERICA

EUROPE

ASIA

JAPAN

AFRICA

SOUTH
AMERICA

AUSTRALIA

Peter & Connie R

First published in Great Britain by Heinemann Library
Halley Court, Jordan Hill, Oxford OX2 8EJ
a division of Reed Educational and Professional Publishing Ltd.
Heinemann is a registered trademark of Reed Educational & Professional Publishing Limited.

OXFORD MELBOURNE AUCKLAND KUALA LUMPUR
SINGAPORE IBADAN NAIROBI KAMPALA JOHANNESBURG
GABORONE PORTSMOUTH NH CHICAGO

Designed by AMR
Illustrations by Art Construction
Printed in Hong Kong / China

02 01 00 99
10 9 8 7 6 5 4 3 2 1

ISBN 0 431 08324 X
This title is also available in a hardback library edition (ISBN 0 431 08315 0).

British Library Cataloguing in Publication Data

Roop, Peter
  A visit to Japan
  1. Japan – Social conditions – 1945 – – Juvenile literature
  2. Japan – Geography – Juvenile literature
  3. Japan – Social life and customs – 1945 – – Juvenile literature
  I.Title II.Japan
  952·.049

Acknowledgements
The Publishers would like to thank the following for permission to reproduce photographs:
J Allan Cash Ltd: pp9, 12, 16, 18; Colorific!: de Marcillac p28; B Glinn-Magnum p20; Hutchison Library:
J Burbank pp5, 22, 24, 29, R Francis p23, M Harvey pp10, 11, M MacIntyre p13; Images Colour Library:
pp 8, 14, 15, 21, 25; JNTO: p26; Panos Pictures: J Holmes pp6, 7, 19; Trip: C McCooey p27

Cover photograph reproduced with permission of P Rauter, Trip

Every effort has been made to contact copyright holders of any material reproduced in this
book. Any omissions will be rectified in subsequent printings if notice is given to the Publisher.

Any words appearing in bold, **like this**, are explained in the Glossary.

Contents

Japan

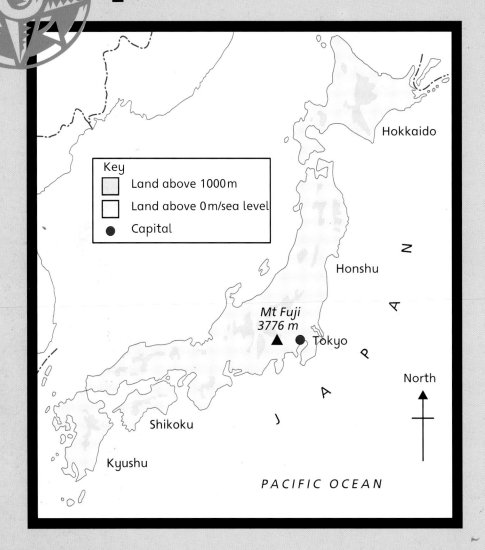

Key
- Land above 1000 m
- Land above 0 m/sea level
- ● Capital

Hokkaido

Honshu

Mt Fuji
3776 m

▲ ● Tokyo

JAPAN

North

Shikoku

Kyushu

PACIFIC OCEAN

Japan is an island country in Asia.
The Japanese call their country Nippon,
which means land of the rising sun.

There are 4000 islands in Japan. Most people live on the four biggest islands. They are Hokkaido, Honshu (above), Shikoku and Kyushu.

Land

Japan has many mountains and **volcanoes**. Some of the volcanoes **erupt**. Also, Japan has about 1500 **earthquakes** each year.

Japan stretches out for a long way. The north islands can have snow while the south islands are still warm. All of the islands have **typhoons**.

Landmarks

Mount Fuji is Japan's most famous mountain. Mount Fuji is a **volcano**. It has not **erupted** for hundreds of years.

Tokyo is the **capital** and Japan's largest city. One out of every ten Japanese lives in Tokyo.

Homes

Most people live in small flats in crowded cities. Most of the cities are on the lowlands near the coast.

In the country, the homes are made of wood. They are only one or two storeys high. The Japanese always take their shoes off before entering the home.

Food

The Japanese enjoy making their food look attractive. They eat small portions of many different types of food but **noodles** are a favourite fast food.

At home, the Japanese sit on the floor and eat from low wooden tables. They use **chopsticks** for all their food. Rice and hot tea are served at every meal.

Clothes

Most Japanese wear clothes like yours
but they wear kimonos on special days.
Farmers wear **traditional** work clothes,
like baggy trousers and straw hats.

Kimonos are long silk robes which are tied with a large sash. There is a different kimono for each season. The light, summer ones are called yukata.

Work

Only a few Japanese are farmers but they grow most of Japan's food. They grow rice, wheat, soybeans, tea, fruit and vegetables. They also keep pigs and chickens.

Japan's fishermen are very successful.
Only China catches more fish in one
year. Most people in Japan work in
offices or factories.

Transport

The bullet train is the fastest way to travel on land. It travels at a speed of 270 kilometres per hour. There is a rail link between two of the islands through the world's longest tunnel.

So many people travel to work by train or **subway** that passengers are pushed onto them by station workers! Airports and motorways link all the main cities.

Language

When Japanese people greet each other they bow to show **respect**. They speak very politely to each other.

It takes a long time to learn to read and write Japanese. There are 1850 **characters** which are written in columns from right to left.

School

Children go to school from the age of
6 to 15. They learn Japanese, maths,
English, physical education and art.
They also practise **earthquake drills**.

Even the young students study very hard. Each night they do hours of homework and extra lessons. They work hard to get into a good college.

Free time

Sumo wrestling is Japan's national sport. Each wrestler has to throw the other one out of the ring. Millions of Japanese also enjoy baseball.

Many Japanese regularly visit parks and gardens. A favourite time to go is in the spring when the cherry trees are in blossom.

Celebrations

Japan has many festivals but New Year is the biggest. It is like a giant birthday party when everyone adds on another year to their age.

Children's Day is celebrated on May 5. Every family flies a **carp** kite or **windsock** for each child.

The Arts

The Japanese have many **traditional crafts** like ink painting, flower arranging or making beautiful pottery. Origami is the art of making models by folding paper.

Noh theatre is only found in Japan.
Actors wear masks to perform **ancient**
stories. Musicians are also on stage and
in costume, to **accompany** them.

Factfile

Name	Japan is its full name.
Capital	The **capital** of Japan is Tokyo.
Languages	Most Japanese speak and write Japanese, but some can also speak Korean or English.
Population	There are about 125 million people living in Japan.
Money	Instead of the dollar or the pound, the Japanese have the yen.
Religions	Most Japanese believe in Buddhism (which is a self-improvement religion) and Shintoism (which includes the worship of spirits). There are also a few Christians, too.
Products	Japan produces lots of rice, fish, steel, cameras, televisions, radios, ships, cars, chemicals and toys.

Words you can learn

ee-chee (ee-tchee)	one
nee (nee)	two
sahn (san)	three
konnichi wa (kon-nee-tchee-wa)	hello
sayonara (sah-yoh-nah-rah)	goodbye
arigato (aree-gah-toh)	thank you
hai (hi)	yes
iie (ee-eh)	no
okaasan (oh-kah-san)	respected mother
otoosan (oh-taw-san)	respected father

Glossary

accompany	to play an instrument while someone else sings or speaks
ancient	from a long time ago
capital	the city where the government is based
carp	a kind of fish like a large goldfish
characters	the symbols or letters in the alphabet
chopsticks	a pair of sticks held in one hand to lift food to the mouth
crafts	skills in making things
drills	a safety routine where people practise what to do when there is a danger, like a fire or an earthquake
earthquake	violent shaking of the ground
erupt	throw out ash and melted rock
noodles	long ribbons made from flour and water, which are then cooked
respect	to value someone or think highly of them
subway	trains that run underground through tunnels
traditional	the way things have been done or made for a long time
typhoons	violent storms with strong winds and heavy rain
volcano	a mountain or hole in the ground that sometimes throws out ash or melted rock from beneath the Earth's surface
windsock	a piece of cloth that blows in the wind

Index